Phillip Phillips

ABDO
Publishing Company

Big
Buddy BOOKS
Buddy Bios

by **Sarah Tieck**

Published by ABDO Publishing Company, PO Box 398166, Minneapolis, Minnesota 55439.

Printed in the United States of America, North Mankato, Minnesota.
102013
012014

 PRINTED ON RECYCLED PAPER

Coordinating Series Editor: Rochelle Baltzer
Contributing Editors: Megan M. Gunderson, Bridget O'Brien, Marcia Zappa
Graphic Design: Maria Hosley
Cover Photograph: *AP Photo*: Amy Sussman/Invision.
Interior Photographs/Illustrations: *AP Photo*: The Albany Herald, Joe Bellacomo (p. 6), Robb Cohen/Robbs Photos/
   Invision (p. 25), Scott Gries (p. 27), Arthur Mola/Invision (p. 13), Danny Moloshok (p. 17), John Shearer/Invision
   (p. 19), Jordan Strauss/Invision (p. 5); *Getty Images*: FOX via Getty Images (pp. 11, 15), David Livingston
   (p. 21), Jim Quinn via Getty Images (p. 6), Rebecca Sapp/WireImage (p. 29), John Sleezer/Kansas City Star/MCT
   via Getty Images (p. 23), Chris Walter/WireImage (p. 9), Kevin Winter (pp. 9, 17).

Library of Congress Cataloging-in-Publication Data

Tieck, Sarah, 1976- author.
  Phillip Phillips : American Idol winner / Sarah Tieck.
     pages cm -- (Big buddy biographies)
  ISBN 978-1-62403-200-4
1. Phillips, Phillip, 1990---Juvenile literature. 2. Singers--United States--Biography--Juvenile literature. I. Title.
  ML3930.P463T54 2014
  782.42164092--dc23
  [B]
                          2013030845

Contents

Rising Star

Phillip Phillips is a singer and songwriter. He is known as a winner of *American Idol*. He has **released** popular songs. And, he has been **interviewed** in magazines and on television.

Phillip won the eleventh season of *American Idol* in 2012. Millions of people watch this television show and vote for their favorite singers.

Leesburg is a very small town. Fewer than 3,000 people live there!

Leesburg City Limit

"A Community on the Grôw"

WELCOME TO
CITY OF LEESBURG
HOME OF
LUKE BRYAN
AND
BUSTER POSEY

AND
PHILLIP
PHILLIPS!

When *American Idol* visited Leesburg, Phillip's parents joined him for a parade.

Tennessee

North Carolina

South Carolina

Alabama

Georgia
● Leesburg

Florida

GULF OF MEXICO

ATLANTIC OCEAN

N W E S

Family Ties

Phillip LaDon Phillips Jr. was born in Leesburg, Georgia, on September 20, 1990. His parents are Sheryl and Phillip Sr. He has two older sisters, LaDonna and Lacey. Phillip grew up in Leesburg and nearby Sasser. His family owned a **pawnshop**.

Early Years

Phillip enjoyed music from a young age. When he was 14, he learned to play the **guitar**. Lacey's boyfriend, Ben Neil, taught him.

Phillip loved playing the guitar. He often practiced along with the family's **karaoke** machine. He learned some classic rock songs.

Phillip learned to play songs by Ozzy Osbourne (*left*) and Deep Purple (*above*) on the guitar.

After a couple years, Phillip formed a band with Lacey and Ben. They **performed** at churches and other places. At first, Phillip just played **guitar**. Then, Lacey and Ben heard him sing and noticed his talent. Soon, Phillip began singing onstage.

At first, singing for an audience made Phillip very nervous. In time, it got somewhat easier.

Building a Name

Phillip attended school while working on his music. After finishing high school, he started studying at Albany Technical College in Georgia.

Phillip and Ben **performed** as often as they could. They played at festivals and other events. They enjoyed it so much that they often just played for a meal or for free.

At Albany Tech, Phillip learned about electronics, motors, pumps, and other types of industrial systems.

13

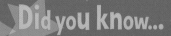
In 2011, Phillip was working for his family's shop. He was also **performing** whenever he got the chance.

Phillip's family and friends encouraged him to try out for *American Idol*. So, he took time off work. He made it through tryouts and became a finalist!

On *American Idol*, Phillip had his own performing style. People came to know him for his low voice and his guitar playing.

American Idol

American Idol is a popular television show. Each season, young people **compete** to be named the best singer. The show has changed since the first season. There have been new winners and new judges.

Thousands of people across the country **audition** for the show. Judges choose a small group of finalists to **perform**. Every week, each finalist sings and then viewers vote. Singers with the fewest votes leave the show. Finally, one winner is chosen.

Steven Tyler, Jennifer Lopez, and Randy Jackson (*left to right*) were the show's judges for season 11. They talked about each performance before viewers voted.

Phillip (*second from right*) quickly became a top contestant.

American Idol Winner

During the show, Phillip learned a lot about **performing**. He sang songs by Creedence Clearwater Revival and Otis Redding. Viewers loved Phillip's strong voice. When they voted, he was the winner!

After he won, Phillip was given a record contract. And, he **released** his song "Home" as a single. It quickly became a hit!

Phillip beat Jessica Sanchez. Then, he performed "Home" on the last show.

New Opportunities

After winning *American Idol*, Phillip began recording his first album. He wanted to be included in the creative parts of making the album. So, he wrote or helped write many of the songs.

Phillip had more opportunities to **perform** after *American Idol*. He loved traveling and living the life of a **professional** singer!

"Home" continued to grow more popular. In July 2012, the single went gold. That means it sold more than 500,000 copies. Later it went platinum, which means it sold more than 1 million copies!

Phillip performed during the MLB All-Star Game in 2012.

In November 2012, Phillip's first album was **released**. It is called *The World From the Side of the Moon*.

Some of the album's hit songs were "Home" and "Gone, Gone, Gone." When the album came out, it was number four on the Billboard Top 200 Albums.

TY 2012
2012
Royals
ALL STAR GAME
JULY 10 FOX
STAR GAME 2012
MLB
GAME

A Singer's Life

As a singer and songwriter, Phillip spends time working on his songs. He records them for albums in a studio.

After an album comes out, Phillip works hard to promote it. He appears on television and in magazines. And, he performs live for fans.

Fans often ask Phillip to pose for pictures.

Off the Stage

When Phillip is not working, he spends time in Leesburg with his family. He likes his mom's cooking. She makes chicken pot pie and deer cube for him.

Phillip also likes to help others. In 2013, he worked with DoSomething.org and VH1 Save the Music Foundation. They gave money for school music education programs.

In 2012, Phillip performed to raise money for people who suffered after Hurricane Sandy.

Buzz

In 2013, Phillip went on tours with John Mayer and Matchbox 20. He also was the **headliner** in a tour that visited colleges.

Phillip's opportunities continue to grow and change. Fans are excited for more music from Phillip Phillips!

In 2013, Phillip sang during An Evening with Phillip Phillips at the GRAMMY Museum.

Snapshot

⭐ **Name**: Phillip LaDon Phillips Jr.

⭐ **Birthday**: September 20, 1990

⭐ **Birthplace**: Leesburg, Georgia

⭐ **Album**: *The World From the Side of the Moon*

⭐ **Appearance**: *American Idol*

Important Words

audition (aw-DIH-shuhn) to give a trial performance showcasing personal talent as a musician, a singer, a dancer, or an actor.

compete to take part in a contest between two or more persons or groups.

guitar (guh-TAHR) a stringed musical instrument played by strumming.

headline to be the main act in a show.

interview to ask someone a series of questions.

karaoke (kehr-ee-OH-kee) a form of entertainment where people sing along to popular music.

pawnshop a shop where people buy and sell objects of value. People can also borrow money by leaving a valuable object at the shop until they repay the money.

perform to do something in front of an audience. A performance is the act of doing something, such as singing or acting, in front of an audience.

professional (pruh-FEHSH-nuhl) working for money rather than only for pleasure.

promote to help something become known.

release to make available to the public.

Web Sites

To learn more about Phillip Phillips, visit ABDO Publishing Company online. Web sites about Phillip Phillips are featured on our Book Links page. These links are routinely monitored and updated to provide the most current information available.

www.abdopublishing.com

Index